Reviews of *Starting a Micro Business*

When my son started his teen business—which he eventually sold in a million dollar deal—he had little knowledge about how to structure it and handle the tax side. It was Carol Topp who helped him learn how to set up his business, keep records and plan for future growth. Chris S.

Carol Topp's books not only helped me launch a successful micro business, but gave me the ability to run my business in an organized, professional manner. She has a simple, instructive, helpful writing style that is easy to understand and execute. The books have helped me accomplish one of the greatest goals I could ever achieve. Jade B., age 16

The book was amazing! With it I am making double minimum wage and I'm not even old enough to work at McDonald's or Kroger! The book has taught me that I don't have to be 15 to have a job! *Starting a Micro Business* has taught me how to manage my time and money wisely between my business, school, and other activities. Ethan E., age 14

Starting a Micro Business is the first business planning resource that I have seen that is geared specifically for teens who are thinking of starting a business. It is a great resource to help a teenager to learn about business and to ultimately start their own business. I strongly recommend this book and its very practical, doable approach to any aspiring young entrepreneur. I think it is provides teens a great first step into the entrepreneurial world. Michael P. Licata, Ph.D, Accounting Professor Villanova University,

Starting a Micro Business

by

Carol Topp, CPA

Ambassador Publishing
Cincinnati, Ohio

ISBN 978-0-9829245-0-1

Scripture taken from THE HOLY BIBLE, NEW INTERNATIONAL VER-
SION® Copyright © 1973, 1978, 1984 International Bible Society.
Used by permission of Zondervan.

Cover Design: Dave Huff
Author Photo: Cathy Lyons

This book is dedicated

to my family: Dave, Emily, and Sarah;

to my teenage micro business clients,

Phillip, Lucas, Emily, Matthew, Lauren, Meghan,

and many more,

to Amanda Bennett,

who encouraged me from the start,

to all the homeschool families

who told me they wanted this book

and to the Lord.

Table of Contents

Introduction
What's Different About
This Book?

I wrote this book because I knew that teenagers needed it. As a mother of two teenagers, I have met plenty of students that wanted to make some money, but didn't know how to get started. I also met a few ambitious students who did make serious money by creating websites and mowing grass, but they needed help with business issues. I started searching for books to help these teenagers.

I didn't like what I found.

There are plenty of books for kids who want to start a business like a lemonade stand. They are geared toward children who are just playing at running a business. They are usually cute books that explain the difference between quarters and dollars and how a bank is a safe place to put your money.

That's necessary information for children, but teenagers need more.

There are plenty of books for people wanting to be entrepreneurs. They are usually geared toward young adults just out of college. The assumption in these books is that the reader can get a bank loan (most teenagers cannot) or that the reader has plenty of time to devote to starting a business.

These books do not consider that a teenager needs to do homework, eat, sleep and still have a social life.

Finally, I ran across a few (but very few) books for teenage entrepreneurs. Some were books written for adults that were repackaged for teenagers by substituting a few words here and there. They were full of unrealistic ideas. I found one book that recommended a teenager open a restaurant! As if a teenager has the time (or money) to run a restaurant! Other books were full of inspiring stories about teen entrepreneurs, but they left me feeling intimidated because the teenagers featured were so very successful.

Their stories seemed beyond the grasp of a normal American teenager.

Some of the information in these books was useful, but they were inadequate in many areas. Few covered business plans. Even fewer discussed taxes in an intelligent and helpful way. There were rarely examples of how to keep good records and very few real life examples.

So I wrote this book because I knew that teenagers needed it.

This book is geared toward teenagers and their lives. There are no unrealistic expectations of opening a restaurant. There are ideas of businesses that real teenagers have started and run successfully. I provide a lot of examples of teenagers I know personally. I walk you though some very important topics such as making a plan and avoiding debt.

That's how this book is different!

This book is very practical. If you want inspiration, it's here in small bites, but primarily this book will be helpful and useful to you. Think of it as getting a CPA's advice for under $20.00!

Chapter One
What is a Micro Business?

Have you heard the term "micro business? Probably not, but you can imagine what it means. It is a very small business—smaller than a small business. The Small Business Administration, a branch of the United States federal government, defines a small business as having up to 1,500 employees and annual income of $25 million, or more in some cases. That's not very small, in my opinion.

Micro Businesses Are Popular
Micro business may not be a familiar term, but micro businesses are very common. MicrobusinessStrategies.com reports that:
- 1 in 8 adults in America own a micro business (thousands of teenagers too!).
- 95% of all American businesses can be classified as micro businesses (fewer than 10 employees).
- 90% of businesses have fewer than 5 employees.
- There are over 25 million micro businesses in America.

- At least 49% (more likely 56%) of all businesses are home based.

Characteristics of Micro Businesses

Micro businesses are quite different from small businesses in several ways:

- Simple and fast to start up
- Only one worker, the owner
- Sole proprietorship (only one owner, unlike a partnership or corporation)
- Little start up money needed or completely debt free
- Usually home-based
- Low risk
- Manageable
- Learn while earning

Emily teaches piano lessons to seven students for 30 minutes each week. The three-and-a-half hours a week is not a heavy load, but she is a busy high school student. She charges $8 for a half hour lesson, a very reasonable price, but twice the hourly rate that she would make working fast food.

Simple and Fast Start Up

Micro businesses are simple businesses that can be started very quickly. They are a perfect business alternative for teenagers because they are small and quite manageable. A teenager should be able to run a micro business while keeping up with school work and extracurricular activities. Running a micro business should only take a few hours a week, up to 20 at most. The time commitment should be similar to working a part time job, but the rewards are much greater!

One Worker

Most micro businesses have only one worker—the owner. The Small Business Administration defines a small business by using a size standard based on the number of employees. Small business can have up to 1,500 employees and still be considered a small business. Micro business owners think differently. They usually operate with no employees, or not many. Frequently, the owner is the only worker. Some micros may hire independent contractors to do a specific task, such as web design, marketing or accounting, but they are not employees.

Why do micros avoid hiring employees? Usually, it is to stay flexible. Micros can start quickly and can also close down quickly. If a teenager needs to shut down his micro, he does not want employees dependent on the business for their livelihood.

Lucas, a 17-year-old micro business owner, called me and explained that his lawn mowing business had grown. He needed to hire a few friends to mow grass for his clients when he could not do it. We discussed the paperwork and taxes involved in hiring employees. Lucas learned a lot about several federal and state agencies. He could handle the paperwork because his employees worked during the summer when Lucas had more time to devote to his business.

Some micros avoid employees because of the added expense and paperwork. Hiring even only one employee means collecting and paying payroll taxes, dealing with the Internal Revenue Service, Social Security Administration, state taxation departments, unemployment, and workers' compensation agencies. Most teenage micro business owners have other priorities and demands on their time, such as homework, and find the burden of employees is more responsibility than they wish to carry.

Sole Proprietorship

Micro businesses usually start as sole proprietorships, meaning one and only one owner, and stay that way until they close operations or are sold. The sole proprietorship is the easiest and fastest method to create a business. There are no contracts to negotiate as with partnerships, nor lawyers to hire as with corporations. Usually, the most micro business owners need to do is acquire a vendor's license if they are selling products or offering a taxable service. Some micros also file a DBA (Doing Business As) name registration with their state or county. An internet search on "start a small business" and a state name will lead to specific state requirements. An Employer Identification Number (EIN) from the Internal Revenue Service and a business checking account are also recommended. My book, *Running a Micro Business,* has more details on these topics.

Most small business owners agonize over their business structure. There are several possibilities including partnership, which has two or more owners, or a corporation, which has several owners who are called shareholders. A micro business owner might ask, "Should my business be a sole proprietorship or a corporation?" or wonder, "Should my business forge a partnership with others?" These are important decisions for a small business owner, but a micro business owner does not worry about her business structure because the sole proprietorship option works best.

Little Start-Up Money Needed

Teenagers love starting micro businesses because little start-up money is needed. Starting a micro business should not mean taking on debt. Micros can be started with equipment the teenager already has at home, such as a computer, a kitchen stove or a piano. Teenagers use knowledge they already possess, such as artistic talent or web design skills.

Starting a micro business should not mean taking on debt.

If start-up funds are needed, there are several ways to raise the cash. Some students work a temporary job to

Lauren worked in retail during the Christmas season to earn start-up funds of $800. With her earnings she paid an accountant to review her business plan and purchased initial inventory.

Matthew started his micro business buying and selling pocket knives at age 12. He borrowed $100 from his parents to buy his first knives and then sold them at enough profit to pay back his loan and buy more knives. The business was launched from there.

19

earn money. The initial start-up funds might go toward advertising or purchasing the first pieces of inventory for resale.

A micro owner can start with a small loan from mom and dad or grandparents. Borrow as little as needed and attempt to pay it back as soon as possible. Other teenagers try selling something to raise initial funds.

In Chapter Five, I discuss the problems with debt and share a lot of ways to get start up money without borrowing it.

Home-Based

Some small businesses feel they have arrived when they have a storefront. They might believe no one will take them seriously without a physical location or office. Today's micro business owners know that a storefront is not necessary for making money. A building or rented space can be a drain on finances and kill a business. Micro businesses are usually home-based, with no physical location. This allows tremendous flexibility if the owner moves or starts college away from home.

Web site owner, Phil, started his business while in high school. When he started college, he rented two dorm rooms, one to sleep in and one for his office (with a desk, two computers, and three monitors), so he could continue to operate his website while attending college.

Low Risk

While I was describing a workshop to a convention coordinator, she said, "Let's call it Teen Entrepreneur." "No," I explained, "Let's call it Micro Business for Teenagers, instead." The difference is important. The word entrepreneur comes from French and means "to undertake or start something new." That definition fits most micro business owners, but today, the word entrepreneur also means taking risks, being an inventor, or having grandiose dreams. One definition I read said an entrepreneur must be a risk-taker, try new things, and create a new business.

But it is not necessary to be a risk-taker to start a micro business. Teenage micro business owners do not want to take risks; they are in business to learn something and to earn money. Starting a business does not need to be risky. Certainly, some micro owners are entrepreneurial in spirit and risk-takers, but not all micro owners are entrepreneurs. As I stated earlier, micro business owners have a purpose—to learn—and usually have a financial goal for their micro.

Starting a micro business does not need to be risky.

There is a misconception that teenagers starting a business must be on the road to greatness and have Microsoft founder, Bill Gates, as their idol. This emphasis on super-success can be intimidating to a teenager just trying to learn the ropes. Instead, micro businesses can be quite simple. It can offer a tried-and-true method for teenagers to earn cash, such as mowing lawns and babysitting.

Some teens fear starting a business because they feel in-

21

adequate. "I'm not an entrepreneur. I didn't invent any-thing," my daughter told me when we discussed means to make money. "You don't have to be an entrepreneur or an inventor," I explained. "Just offer a service that people want." Emily offered piano lessons. She did not invent anything new. She used the piano that sat in our living room and taught from the piano books that she already owned.

A micro business does not have to create a new product or an invention.

Manageable

Micro businesses stay small so they are manageable for a busy teenage owner. Frequently business owners seem to focus on growth and expansion. "Grow your business. Get more clients. Make more money. More, more, more!" We hear it all the time in books, maga-zines, and websites geared toward small business own-ers. The assumption that every business needs to be constantly pushing and grab-bing for more is not the micro business way.

Emily had seven piano students at one point, but found that five students was more manageable. She said, "I could take on a few more students, but I would need to give up something else. This is enough for now, and teaching five students gives me enough spending money."

A micro business owner has a manageable business and priorities in life. For teenage micro owners, a high priority is being a student. If they are religious, their top priorities include service to God and time with their family. Their micro business is a means to an end, such as making a car payment, but not the end itself. Micro business owners stay balanced. They don't let life spiral out of control. They learn to say, "No more. I have a life. This is enough for now."

Micro business owners aim to be content when they have achieved their goals. They understand the value of a manageable, balanced life.

> ***Drive thy business, let not that drive thee.***
> Benjamin Franklin

Purpose: Learn and Earn
The main purpose of a micro business is to learn while earning money. Micro owners are interested in learning everything they can about running a business. They intend to make money from their micro, but learning is paramount in their minds. Matthew, the knife-seller, says that he learned more from running his business than he did in school!

Yara was homeschooled and started a micro business offering babysitting during the day. Her goal for the micro business was to pay for her horseback riding lessons.

Linnea has a goal to visit her homeland of China and started two micro businesses: teaching Chinese and making and selling jewelry to save up for her trip.

The goal is to learn and earn

Running a micro will teach you to:
- manage time
- serve customers
- overcome shyness
- be unique
- track income and expenses
- express yourself
- gain confidence
- balance commitments
- overcome fear
- Marketing a product or service
- multi-task
- and much more

It might be overwhelming to be stretched by doing new things, but it can also be exciting as you grow in confidence and success. Here is some encouraging advice from the Bible that the apostle Paul gave to his student, Timothy.

> *Don't let anyone look down on you for being young. Instead, make your speech, behavior, love, faith, and purity an example for other believers.*
> I Timothy 4:12

Benjamin Franklin had some wise words to say about learning and acquiring knowledge.

> *An investment in knowledge always pays the best interest.*
> Benjamin Franklin

Some micro business owners see their businesses as a launching point for another business. They take what they learned from running a micro and start another business, adding to their knowledge as they go.

Some micro owners have a specific financial goal for their business. Perhaps it is to buy a car, pay the insurance and fill it with gas. Many students run a micro business to help pay for a hobby, a trip, or college, while others feed a love for music, iTunes, or text messages.

Is a micro business for you? It is a great launching point for many teenagers who want to learn how to run a business and earn some money, while maintaining their priorities. The following chapters will help you learn what you need to get started, avoid problems, and be successful. I have included many more stories from other teenage micro business owners so that you can be inspired and encouraged.

Phil was in high school when he discovered that he was good at buying small websites, revamping them, building up traffic and then reselling the site for a profit. After a few years of running his business as a micro, Phil launched a larger website project using the profits from his micro business. He learned how to hire web designers, advertise on the internet, and even how to pay taxes on his profit! After only two years, he was offered $300,000 for his website.

Important Points

Micro businesses are different in several ways:
- Simple and fast to start up
- Only one worker, the owner
- Sole proprietorship (one owner)
- Little start up money needed or completely debt free
- Usually home-based
- Low risk
- Manageable
- Learn while earning

Chapter Two
Getting an Idea
A Collection of Micro Business Ideas Best for Teenagers

A Good Micro Business

What's a good micro business for a teenager? As the mother of two teenagers and an accountant who advises micro business owners, I think a successful micro business needs to have these qualities:

Low start up cost. I do not like debt or loans, so the start-up needs to be self-funded. How can you get the money to start a micro business? Sell something, work at another job to earn the start-up cash, or negotiate a *small* loan from your parents. By small, I mean a loan that you could pay back in less than three months or by having only a handful of customers or sales.

Low risk. You are in this to make money, not to lose it! Risky businesses are for people with plenty of experience in running a business, but not for your first venture.

Balanced. You should be able to run a micro business without losing your life to it. You have a life—you are a full-time student. You should be able to get your homework finished, be involved in sports and church youth group and still run a micro business. Life is more than working on your business. Keep a balance.

Home-based or transportation provided. I love it when the parents pick up my daughter for her babysitting jobs; one family even let my 17-year-old drive their extra car for two weeks while she was their nanny. An ideal micro business can be run from your home or at least not cause a transportation headache for your family.

Use skills and talent. Many lists of business opportunities are out of reach for most teenagers because they lack the experience or skills. You will get there in time, but most teenagers need to grow in experience. It is best to stick to something you know well, like computers, algebra, or music.

Ideas for Micro Businesses

I have browsed through hundreds of small business ideas to bring you these micro business ideas that are best for teenagers. I once read a list of business ideas for teenagers, and it listed "run a restaurant" as if that is a reasonable idea for a teenager who needs to go to school, do homework, and still eat and sleep! The ideas I share are all possible for a busy teenager. I personally (or virtually) know of teenagers running every one of these types of businesses, so I know that they work.

A word of caution: ***Do not be too hasty to reject some of these ideas.***

No one likes any job that has the word "cleaning" in it, but you will not be doing it for the rest of your life. Your first micro business may be a temporary business, but it could help accomplish your goal to learn something and make money doing it.

Also realize that you may not have this business for a very long time. Micro businesses are easy to start and they are easy to close

Russ has two broken lawn mowers in his garage. He offered them to his son for a micro business. "Fix these up and start a business to sell them," he encouraged his son, Brady. Brady might only work on those two lawn mowers and then close the business if he does not care for the work. On the other hand, he may find out he is good at lawn mower repair and keep the business going.

down. Many teenagers only run their business in the summer, or only run it for a few months.

Now on to the ideas:

Art lessons. Offer a few private or group art classes to younger children. Let them paint, sculpt with clay, or make paper mache. The messier the project, the more the parents will love you for doing the clean up (and pay you for it)!

Artist. Use your skills to paint or draw portraits of people, houses, or pets—the more personal the better. Charge an additional fee to mat and frame the drawing.

Author. Write articles for magazines in print or on the web and get paid. Start by reading some books about writing for magazines. Consider writing your own book and self publish it. Electronic books—eBooks—are a quick and easy way to sell what you write. See Chapter Six for links to get you started on self publishing.

One student made her babysitting micro business unique by advertising to neighbors that she was hosting a regular babysitting service every Tuesday evening from 6:00 to 8:00 pm in her home. Her customers could plan ahead knowing they had babysitting that evening.

Babysitting. The time-honored profession of teenagers is babysitting. Put a unique twist on your business by adding extra services such as laundry, chauffeur, pet-walking or light housecleaning for an extra fee. Offer a short timeframe of childcare, such as two to three hours on a regular basis. Parents can use the time for running errands or going out. Watch several children at once to maximize your profit.

Baking. Many people will hire someone to bake something as simple as cupcakes! There are several zoning and health regulations when preparing food for resale, so check with your local county extension office to learn your local area regulations. Chapter Six has some helpful information and links.

Bookkeeping. If you've taken a basic accounting class, you can do some bookkeeping. You can charge a higher rate if you learn an accounting package like Quick-Books. Visit your library or local bookstore for information on the software, or your local community college may offer classes. There are also on-line Quick-Books training classes—some for free! Find them by doing an internet search on "learn QuickBooks on-line".

Candy making. Similar to the baking, but candy making may have different health requirements that are easier to live with. Box them up nicely and candy can make an excellent gift.

Hannah makes luscious buckeye candies every Christmas and pockets a nice profit. Buckeyes are peanut butter balls dipped in chocolate. Yum!

A single idea/the sudden flash of a thought/may be worth a million dollars.

Robert Collier, author of self help books

Car-detailing. Wash, wax and vacuum the inside of cars and minivans. Do it like the professionals. Offer to go to the customer's home for an additional fee.

Catering. You can offer to work under a professional caterer to learn the ropes before you launch your own business. Health regulations are strict when it comes to food preparation, so be sure to read the section in Chapter Six on preparing food at home for resale.

Cleaning. Houses, garages, yards and cars all need to be cleaned at some point. You could be the person that gets paid for doing it! It may be hard work and you will get messy, but cleaning pays very well.

> Kalief Rollins sells a T-shirt that reads "Caution: Educated African American Male." He won a $10,000 grand prize from the National Youth Entrepreneurship Competition for his micro business.

Clothing. Screen printing T-shirts, shorts or sweat pants can be very profitable, especially if you come up with a catchy phrase. Some teenagers make clothing for others to try out fashion design as a career. You can sell your designs locally or on-line.

Computer Help Desk. Be on call from your home or, for an additional fee, make house calls to sick computers. Or just answer simple questions about popular software like iTunes. You may be surprised at what people will pay to get basic help with their computers. A friend of mine installed Microsoft Vista and could not find the Print command for two weeks!

My daughters and I needed help to straighten out our iTunes library after I accidentally deleted all the music on my iPod. I have a friend, Dave, that started a micro business doing computer support. Dave spent an hour in front of our PC answering our stupid questions like, "What do the blue circles mean?" and "What do the checkmarks mean?" Then he showed us a neat feature called smart playlists to help get us organized. You may already have some computer knowledge that can be turned it into a profitable micro business.

Computer set up. What may be easy for you is intimidating to some people, and they would gladly pay you to run cables and load software.

Computer tutor. If you are a patient teacher, there are plenty of people who would love to have a teenager show them how to better use their computers. My daughter is taking a Photoshop class, and she already has three adults that want her to show them how Photoshop works. If she goes to their house, she'll charge a

One teenage boy made $300 by making friendship bracelets in his high school colors and selling them at football games. They were so popular he needed his little sister to help make bracelets to meet the demand.

premium price.

Crafts. Scout out craft shows to see what the latest and best selling craft items are, and then use your talent to make some cash. You do not have to rent a booth at a craft show, but instead go to where your market is- like school, your neighborhood, or the soccer field.

De-clutter: Do you love HGTV shows on organization? You might be able to find someone to hire you to de-clutter their house like you see on TV.

Decorative painting. Learn One Stroke ™ painting from the TV show or books at the library and then paint walls, chairs, or furniture. Take photographs of every painting job to show customers what you can do for them.

eBay assistant: Offer to sell your neighbors' stuff on eBay and take a cut for yourself. Combine the de-cluttering, garage sale and eBay tasks into a full package to help your neighbors profit from their excess stuff.

It seems like once people grow up, they have no idea what's cool.

Bill Watterson, cartoon artist of *Calvin & Hobbes*

Editor. My daughter was a whiz at grammar, while I was not, so she edited my articles and books until she went off to college. Offer your editing services to aspiring authors, fellow students, or small business owners wanting to send a newsletter to customers. Show off your ability by doing a sample edit of a page or two first.

Elder care or companion. I know of teenagers who "babysit" elderly people who go to bed by 7:00 or 8:00 pm. It gives the caretaking family an evening out that is much appreciated and you can even get your homework done after your "client" has gone to bed.

Freezer meal service. Offer to cook full meals and freeze them for a busy mom. Be careful to follow local ordinances on food preparation. Your local county extension or 4-H office will have information on food safety in a business. Chapter Six has several links.

Gardening. My friend's children were hired by a real estate agent to pull weeds for houses she was trying to sell. Maybe you could get a job like that.

Garage sale assistant: Advertise, organize, and run a garage sale for your neighbors. Get several neighbors together and really earn the bucks!

Gift Baskets. Assemble baskets for graduation or teenage birthdays, since you know what teenagers like to get as gifts!

House sitting. Collect mail, water the plants, and look after the property of a neighbor who is on vacation.

Mother's helper. This position is less responsibility than babysitting because the mother usually stays in the house. This is a great business to start if you need more experience working with children or babies. You may be paid less than a babysitter, but you will learn as you earn!

Music accompanying. Pianists are in demand as accompanists. My daughter was paid for her time to rehearse and perform as an accompanist to a teenage cello player for his school music competition.

Music lessons. Are you a drummer? Eric, a teenager in Ohio, teaches eight drum students every week. Use your knowledge of any instrument to teach children in a micro business.

Music performance. Some talented musicians are paid to play at weddings or social gatherings. Harpists, violinists, and pianists are the most popular, but don't forget the garage bands that can get paid for playing a gig.

Ideas can be life-changing. Sometimes all you need to open the door is just one more good idea.
Jim Rohn, entrepreneur and author

Organizing. Organize your neighbor's house, playroom, or garage. Charge the customer for bins, tubs, and labels that you purchase and then add on the value of your time. Take before and after photos to use on your advertising fliers.

Painting. Like Tom Sawyer, you could get paid to paint a fence, a shed, or a house or, if you are more artistic, try decorative painting.

Party planning. Plan a birthday party or holiday parties for your neighbors' children.

Pet hotel. Care for other people's pets while they are away from home. Your family could house rabbits, cats, and dogs for friends on vacation.

Pet sitting or dog walking. Walking dogs, cleaning the yard of their messes, and pet sitting for neighbors on vacation are great ideas. There is a grown man in my hometown who charges $10 a yard to clean up after a dog. It is not the nicest job in the world, but a teenager could certainly do it!

Photographer. Take pictures of parties and special events for neighbors. This frees up the hostess to enjoy herself and get in some of the pictures.

Raising and selling livestock or animals. 4-H kids can make a tidy profit doing this. Many of the 4-H kids I know do not even live on a farm. They leave their animals at a nearby farm and drive out regularly to care for the animal.

Scrapbooking. Offer to create a scrapbook on paper (and charge extra for the supplies), or create a digital version if the customer prefers. Combine doing the photography with scrapbook creation for a premium service at a higher fee.

Sewing. I met a teenage girl who was sewing saddle blankets for her fellow horse-lovers and another girl who converted her brother's old jeans into purses. Have you considered sewing baby slings, doll clothes, or Halloween costumes?

Linnea was born in China and adopted by an American family when she was 14. She tutors other adopted Chinese children in their native tongue. It is easy for her to teach simple phrases and songs from China and the parents love it! To save time, she teaches five students at once in a small group.

Tutoring. Teach school subjects, such as math and Spanish, or offer lessons in swimming, music or art. The students may be able to walk to your house for the lesson or vice versa. Charge a premium for going to the student's home. Consider teaching a small group of children at the same time to maximize your income.

Videotaping. Offer to film an important occasion such as a birthday, music recital or sporting event and then create a DVD of the special event. I hired someone to assemble 40 photographs of my family for my parents' 50th wedding anniversary. They put the photos to music and we played it over and over at their anniversary party.

My daughter set up a simple website for a local hair stylist. The owner, who is a computer newbie, was thrilled with the site and paid Sarah well.

Web site development. Build a website for a small business, family, or a nonprofit organization. What is easy to you may be intimidating to a newbie. It doesn't have to be a complicated website; start simple and use some of the free website builder tools offered by webhosts like **1and1.com**.

Yard maintenance. Lawn mowing, mulch spreading, and snow shoveling are great micro business ideas. You may already have the equipment you need to start. If not, purchase only what you need to get started.

Lucas bought his first riding lawnmower at a garage sale when he was 12 with savings from a paper route. As his business grew, he slowly bought more equipment. "Allow your business to grow, and then grow your equipment into your business," he advises.

Avoiding Scams

I usually encourage teenage micro business owners to start their own business and not sell someone else's products.

Occasionally, you may see advertised a product or opportunity that sounds like it might be easier than starting from scratch. There are a lot of people out there willing to take your money, especially on the Internet, so be careful. Be very suspicious of promises of fast money that sound too easy.

Make sure you understand exactly what you would be doing and how you would earn money. If you cannot explain it to your parents, it might be a scam. Ask their opinion and advice. Your parents may see something suspicious that you do not. Trust them; it is their job to protect you and your money!

Here are some clues that you might be dealing with a scam artist:

- They require that you make a minimum purchase to qualify.
- They are not willing to give you their full name and contact information, including a telephone number.
- You are expected to pay before being given a good sample of the product you are expected to sell.
- The program requires you to sell something technical in nature, but says that you do not need technical expertise to sell it.
- There are promises that you will make money without work, experience, or any kind of investment.
- It sounds too good to be true.

- There is only a vague idea of what the job is really all about.
- Several promises of making tremendous amounts of money with little time invested are made.
- The advertising has a lot of exclamation points and lofty promises.
- An online ad is placed on a free web hosting site or uses a free e-mail service (like Yahoo or Gmail).
- No telephone number is given.
- The ads require you to pay a fee to get information or dial a 900 (toll) phone number.
- Working at home is the main emphasis in the ad, not the skills or experience needed to perform the job.
- They pressure you to decide and make a payment quickly.

What's Next?

I hope that some of the ideas in this chapter appeal to you. What you need to do next is consider a few carefully. This checklist will guide you through the next steps.

1. List three or four of your favorite ideas.
2. Discuss them with your parents. Tell your parents you are in the early stages of just exploring an idea. Try not to get discouraged if they see all the pitfalls and none of the potential. Parents are good at protecting you from failure, but may need to work on encouraging your ideas.
3. Read the next chapter on some of the problems

with certain business ideas and implement the suggested solutions when you can.

4. Make up a business plan for one or two ideas that make the cut after talking with your parents.

5. As part of your business plan, start reading about your chosen idea. In Chapter Six, I share some books and websites for particular businesses that should get you started.

6. Developing a business plan may eliminate a few ideas or spark new ones, so stay open to new ideas.

7. Keep reading, learning, and growing.

Important Points

- Look for a micro business that has:
    - Low start up cost
    - Low risk
    - Balance
    - Home-based or transportation provided
    - Use for your skills and talents
- Consider several ideas
- Learn more about each potential idea, including its problems and pitfalls
- Recognize and avoid scams
- Make a business plan to evaluate your idea
- Keep learning, reading, and growing

Chapter Three
Problems and Pitfalls
And How to Avoid Them

There are problems with every business opportunity. Think of the problems that Microsoft faced as a young company. They were trying to build an untested product, a micro computer, with a huge risk of failure. We also know that eventually there were huge payoffs that made Bill Gates the world's richest self-made man. In starting your micro business, you will run into problems, too. This chapter will try to help you see those pitfalls so you can do your best to avoid them.

However, you should not abandon a business idea just because I, or someone else, points out a flaw. What you should do is consider each problem in the planning stage and try to find a solution. I'll help you out with some solutions, but you will probably come up with several clever ideas yourself.

The Problem with Products

When you mention "micro business," many people think of a product to sell. Selling products can be one of the hardest businesses to run successfully. Here's why:

1. Inventory: There are many decisions to consider such as how much to purchase and how to pay for inventory.

2. Storage: You will need a place to store the inventory and also space to wrap, label, and ship the packages.

3. Shipping: It is not cheap to mail products and going to the post office to ship items can be time consuming.

4. Packaging: You will need boxes, envelopes, labels, packaging, etc., all which costs money and takes up space.

5. Unsold inventory: What happens if you bought inventory but cannot sell it?

6. Back Orders: When you run out of inventory, your customers will have to wait until you receive more inventory to ship. Some customers will cancel their orders if they have to wait.

7. Returns: It is impossible to make everyone happy and you will have to deal with returned products. If there is be nothing wrong with the product, you may be able to resell it, but you may be returned a damaged item. Returns can get expensive because you paid for the shipping initially and may have to pay shipping again to mail a replacement.

8. Record keeping: You may need software to help

track your inventory. If you sell more than one or two items, inventory tracking can become too complex to be done on paper or in a spreadsheet. You will probably need to invest in small business accounting software like QuickBooks.

9. End of year count: Your accountant will need to know the value of your inventory at the end of the year in order to prepare your tax return. Allow some time around December 31 to count every item in storage. Be sure you keep good records on what you paid for each item also.

10. Sales tax: You may need to collect sales tax on products you ship. The sales tax rules and rates vary by state and usually by county and city. The sales tax rules are complex and you should keep excellent, detailed records and get advice from an accountant.

Solutions to Problems with Products

There are many solutions to the problems of selling a product. Technology has opened many doors to selling and delivering products that eliminate inventory and shipping problems for a micro business owner. Other solutions involve planning ahead or adjusting your product line so you make the most profit for the smallest effort.

Sell digital products
Cindy Rushton stopped shipping physical copies of her books when her "shipping department" (her son, Matt) left home to join the military. She knew she didn't want

to do the shipping herself; it was too time consuming, so she switched to selling only electronic books. Her customers were happy to get the books immediately via computer download.

> Cynthia owns a Pampered Chef business. She takes customers' orders, but the manufacturer (Pampered Chef) ships the order directly to the customer. Cynthia doesn't have inventory sitting in her home.

Drop shipping

A micro business retailer can use drop shipping to avoid keeping inventory. Drop shipping means that the manufacturer mails the product directly to your customer. You act as the middleman, finding customers and making the sale.

Only order items after a sale is complete

Sonnie runs a screen printing business called **BadOmelet.com** (visit her website to see why she named her business after spoiled food). She can print your name and company logo on just about anything from T-shirts and pens to duct tape! Sonnie has hundreds of items for screen printing in her catalog, but she doesn't keep hundreds of items in her inventory. She only orders items when a customer orders screen printing. She only orders as many items as the customer wants. This keeps her inventory costs low and manageable.

Use a shipping service

Many businesses will hold your inventory and ship your products for you. Print on demand publishers such as **CreateSpace.com** or **Lulu.com** combine the printing and shipping service for books. CreateSpace will also burn CDs and DVDs and ship them to your customers.

Only order inventory one month in advance and plan, plan, plan!

Linda writes and sells books to homeschool families. She knows that most homeschool families buy their books in July, August, and September. She plans ahead to have enough money set aside to make large purchases of inventory from her printer in July.

Give away inexpensive items or roll the product cost into your full service price

Consider offering a low-cost item to customers when they order a higher priced service. For example, if you offer $200 web design services, include a book you wrote on how to write a blog post and increase your price to $215.

Discontinue unprofitable or low profit margin items

I visited a website where a woman was selling cookbooks, kitchen gadgets and cookie cutters. The cookbooks were priced at around $10, but some of the gadgets were only a dollar or two and the cookie cutters were priced at under a dollar. I cannot imagine that she made any profit on these low-priced items. Discarding these items could avoid the inventory problems or she could increase the selling price of the cookbook and include a small gadget or cookie cutter as a free gift when a customer purchases a cookbook.

The Problem with Service Businesses

Micro businesses run by selling either a product or a service. I discussed the problems with products, but selling services can have problems too. Fortunately, the problems with a service-oriented business are usually fewer than businesses with products. Most micro businesses are service-based businesses because the owners find them easier to manage. Some of the problems you might encounter in your service-based business are time management and dealing with customers. Thankfully, there are solutions to these problems.

Time limitations
With a service business, you cannot sell products while you sleep because *you* are the product. It is your time that you are selling, whether it is to babysit, design a website, or give a piano lesson. The limitation of a service business is that there is only one of you to go around and you only have 24 hours in a day. You can only serve a limited number of customers at a time.

Dealing with people
When you are selling your services, you typically deal with your customers on a very personal level. A service-oriented business does not make a quick sale and have the customer walk away. Instead, a micro business owner selling a service must deal with people. Usually this can be fun and very rewarding if you enjoy helping people, but you may run into difficult or demanding customers at times. You may need to learn how to deal with complaints or unhappy customers.

Solutions for Service Businesses

Hire help

If you are too busy to serve all your customers, you may need to hire help. I do not recommend hiring employees. The paperwork, taxes, and management of employees is usually too complex for a teenage micro business owner. Instead, I recommend you hire other micro business owners to help you. You can hire other business owners as independent contractors to update your website, help with marketing, or serve customers when you cannot. Employees and independent contractors can do similar jobs, but they have different legal and tax situations. These issues are discussed more in my book: *Money and Taxes in a Micro Business*.

Pass it along

Pass along the idea of running a micro business to a friend. Encourage another teenager to start a micro business and give him or her the names of a few customers to start them off.

> Alexandria teaches piano lessons to beginning students. She was so popular as a teacher, that she could not take any more students. She encouraged her sister, Juliann, to start teaching piano also. Between the two sisters, they teach 13 students.

Sell your knowledge

Instead of selling your time, which is limited, you can sell what you know as a book, eBook, video, or seminar.

Nick Tart, of **LawnMowingGuide.com** mowed a lot of grass as a teenager. Then he wrote an ebook to tell other teenagers how to run a lawn care business. That's an excellent example of how to sell what you know.

Work smarter, not harder.
Unknown

Increase your price
If you become so busy you cannot handle all your customers, it is time to increase your prices. Higher prices mean that you can take fewer customers and still make plenty of money. Charging a higher price for a common service, like babysitting, may mean you lose some customers, but you should be paid more for every hour you work.

Learn customer service skills
One of the drawbacks to a service-oriented business is dealing with difficult people. You may need to learn how to handle complaints or criticisms. Learning customer service skills can help. In my book, *Running a Micro Business,* Chapter Three Customer Service offers some ideas on serving your customers and dealing with difficult people.

We have two ears and one mouth so we may listen more and talk the less.
Epictetus, Roman philosopher

Listen to what customers want
Many books on customer service emphasize the importance of listening to your customers. By listening carefully, you can learn what your customers want. This

will help you focus on providing services that they really desire and are willing to pay for. For example, Rob offers lawn services and listened when his customers complained about moles digging tunnels in their yards. He added a service to trap moles. It is not a fun task, but homeowners are willing to pay a high price to be rid of moles. He now does more business trapping moles than mowing grass. It is less work and pays better.

The Problem with Partners

Sometimes teenagers are afraid to launch a business by themselves, so they find a partner to join them. Partnership arrangements can be quite informal with only a verbal agreement between people, but the best partnerships have a written agreement, reviewed by a small business lawyer. Be aware that partnerships may involve several problems.

Four ways partnerships can cause problems

1. They are easy to get into and difficult to dissolve. Partnerships are like being married, but you are not in love. Just like a bad marriage, partnerships can include hurt feelings, betrayals, cheating, and self-preservation. Sometimes dissolving a partnership is as complex as a divorce because of the money involved.

2. Unequal. A partnership agreement might state that the profits are split 50/50, but what about the work load or the expenses? It is rarely split evenly. Two teenage boys launched a partnership based on a ver-

bal agreement. The business did well and the boys agreed to spend the profits on each of them buying computers. One boy spent $300, while the other spent $500. Was that equal? No. The boys, who used to be best friends, are no longer in business together, nor are they friends. Unfortunately, a partnership can destroy a friendship.

3. Take upon the debts of another. Like in a marriage, you are responsible for the debts of another person when in a partnership. There is very little you can do if your partner racks up bills while you are trying to be frugal.

4. Tied for life. A partnership dissolves when both partners agree or upon the death of a partner. What if you want out of a partnership agreement, but your partner does not? You are stuck.

This nearly happened to Brent, an entrepreneur with a great idea. He met with me to discuss taxes, but I became confused when he mentioned a partner. "I thought you were a sole proprietor," I asked. "Oh, yeah, well, the guy who did my website never charged me. I thought I'd make him a partner and split the profits." Bad idea. Brent would be stuck in this arrangement long after the web site was paid off. Instead, make an arrangement to pay for services over time as you generate profit, but don't be tied for life.

Avoid partnerships in your micro business. If you lack expertise, hire someone to help you, but avoid entering into a partnership agreement, even on an informal basis. Even verbal agreements can be binding.

We must not promise what we ought not, lest we be called on to perform what we cannot.
Abraham Lincoln

Be careful what you promise to do with others. Things can change, so micro business owners should avoid long term commitments. Also, be careful to trust what others promise you. They may be well-intentioned, but unable to deliver. Get all important or money-related promises in writing. The other party may not want a written agreement. Tell him you are forgetful and need things in writing to recall the details. Then hand him or her a written summary of your agreement. This may not be a full-fledged partnership agreement, but it is at least a written understanding of your arrangement.

Important Points

- All businesses can have problems. Consider potential problems now and try to find a solution.

- Businesses with products have the problem of dealing with inventory.

- Several solutions to product-oriented businesses include drop shipping and selling digital products.

- Service-oriented businesses have problems of limited time.

- Possible solutions for service businesses are to sell your knowledge or hire help.

- Partnerships have many pitfalls for teenage micro business owners.

Chapter Four
Writing a Business Plan

A Business Plan

After you have an idea for your micro business, you should make a plan on paper to help you anticipate anything that might go wrong. By thinking through issues like who will buy your product and how to reach them, you will save time, money, and avoid frustration.

A business plan can be kept short and simple for most micro businesses. A simple business plan should have three main sections and run about five pages. The plan that follows is twelve pages, but that's because it allows room for you to write by hand. If you type in your information, it will only run about five pages as in the example at the end of the chapter.

Business Plan Sections

1. Business Concept
Description of the product or service
Description of the industry
How to measure success

2. Marketing Plan
Potential customers
The competition
Market surveys
Risks

3. Financial Plan
Start up expenses
Cost of your product or service
Price you will charge customers
Break even analysis
Projected income statement

In this chapter, you will create a business plan by answering a series of questions. If you cannot answer the questions, you might need to find some experts to help you.

Start by asking for advice from your parents, an accountant, a current business owner, and potential customers. They can help you with pricing decisions and give you marketing ideas as well; their input will be invaluable to you. Listen to their suggestions as wisdom, not criticisms of your ideas. They want you to succeed.

> 69% of business owners who created a business plan said that it was a major contributor to their success.

Business Plan
for

_____

(name of your micro business)

Business Concept

Product or Service:_____

Describe your product or service:

What makes your product or service unique?

Describe the industry (i.e. pet food, clothing, education, auto repair, retail, food, etc.) and explain the need for your product or service:

What are the new trends in your industry?

Is there opportunity for you in your industry?

How will you measure success? Will it be a financial goal or based on sales/number of customers? Define your goal in numbers (money, people, or sales units): *Example: I want to make enough profit to finance a ski trip in January. The total cost will be $400.*

What do you hope to learn by starting this micro business?

What knowledge, experience, and skills do you possess that will be helpful in your business?

What knowledge do you lack?

List an accountant who can help you:_____

List a lawyer who can help you:_____

List an insurance agent who can help:_____

List an experienced business owner who can guide you:_____

What licenses and permits are required to operate your business?
Examples include EIN (Employer Identification Number) from the IRS, vendor's license, sales tax permit, assumed name registration, zoning permit, or food preparation permit.

Marketing Plan

Customers
Who are your potential customers?

How will you reach potential customers? Where will you find them?

How much will you spend (in time and money) advertising? Be as specific as possible and include website costs.

Competition
Who is your competition?

What are your competitors' strengths? What are your competitors' weaknesses?

How will you stand out? Why will people buy from you and not your competition?

Surveys

Tell at least five people about your product or service. Ask them: Would you buy from me? How much would you pay?

Record what they said:

Name	Would you buy from me?	What price would you pay?

Risks

What are your major areas of risk? What can break? What can go wrong? What money could you lose?

Financial Plan

This may be the hardest part of the business plan to complete. If you need help in any part, see the example that follows. An accountant or a business owner mentor can help.

Start Up Expenses

Equipment
What start up equipment is needed? Will you need a computer, a desk, an oven?

Where will it come from? Does your family already own the equipment? Ask your parents' permission to use it.

Will you need to buy some equipment? What will it cost to purchase?

Equipment Needed	Parental Approval	Own or Need to Buy?	Cost to Buy

Storage
What storage or preparation space is needed? Where will it come from? Does your family have the space? Ask your parents' permission to use it! Will you need to rent space? What will it cost to rent?

Space Needed	Parental Approval	Own or Need to Rent?	Cost to Rent Space

Other Start Up Expenses

What other startup expenses will you have? Get specific costs.

Item	Cost
Advertising	
Professional advice	
Licenses and permits	
Starting inventory	
Supplies	
Other:	
Total Start Up Expenses	

Initial Funding for Start Up Expenses

Where will your initial funding come from? *Examples: your savings, your other job, mom and dad, gifts, investors.*

Source of Start Up Funds	Amount

If you are borrowing money from family or friends, what is the repayment plan? Be specific with dates or milestones and amounts.

Lender	Amount Owed	Payment	Frequency	Pay Off Date

Item Cost

Fixed Costs: List costs that do not vary with the amount of sales. These are spent regardless of how many sales you make.
Examples are your monthly internet charge, loan repayment, cell phone use, rental space, professional advice, advertising, website.

Fixed Costs	Amount each month (or year)
Total Fixed Cost	per month (or year)

Variable Costs (or Cost of Goods Sold): List costs that vary with the amount of sales.

Examples: material to produce your product, merchant fees per sale, shipping and packaging costs. Do not include your own labor. It comes out of your profit. Variable Costs are also called Cost of Goods Sold.

Variable Costs	Amount per unit sold
Total Variable Cost per Unit	per unit

(Repeat as necessary for each unique product)

Profit

What profit do you hope to make on each item sold or customer serviced?
*If you are unsure start by adding 25-50% of the cost to be
your profit.*

Pricing

What will you charge?
*If you are unsure try this equation: 1.25 * Variable Cost per
Unit = $_____/ unit*
(that would be 25% markup on your variable costs)

Is it reasonable?

What do your competitors charge?

Sales

What are your estimated sales for the first three months,
the next three months, and the first year?
*You can start with number of products sold or number of
customers serviced, but then calculate the dollars of sales.*

	Sales in units or customers	Sales in dollars
First 3 months sales		
3-6 months sales		
Sales for first year		

Break-Even Analysis

Add all the Fixed Costs (from above)
      Start Up Expenses $_____
      Fixed Costs $_____

Total Fixed Costs for first year: $_____

Total Variable Costs (from above): $_____

Margin per unit = Selling Price per Unit – Variable Cost per Unit. *This is a measure of how much profit you make for each unit sold.*

    = $_____ – $ _____

    = $_____ per unit

Break-even point = Total Fixed Costs/Margin per Unit. *This is how many units you must sell in the first year to break even.*

= $_____ / $_____ per unit

= _____ units

Is it reasonable? Can you sell that much?

Collect Data

Fill in the gray areas in the chart on the next page with the numbers from your business plan. Calculate the other lines as indicated. See the example that follows for help in filling this out.

Projected Income Statement for First Year

Income
Total Sales (from the chart, Total column) $
Other Income (interest on savings, etc.) $_____
Total Income $

Less Cost of Goods Sold (from the chart)   ($_____)
Gross Profit (Income – COGS) $
Expenses (list separately)
    Start-up costs $
    Advertising $
    Professional advice $
    Supplies $
    Other $
Total Expenses $_____
Net Income (Gross Profit- Expenses) $

	Product #1	Product #2	Product #3	Total
1 Number sold in one year				
2 Selling Price per unit				
3 Variable Cost per unit				
4 Fixed Costs				
5 Margin per unit (Line 2 - Line 3)				
6 Break Even Point in units (Line 4/Line 5)				
7 Total Sales (Line 1 * Line 2)				
8 Total COGS(Line 1 * Line 3)				
9 Gross Profit (Line 7 – Line 8)				

What's Next?

Now that you have completed your business plan, you should show it to at least three people: your parents, an accountant, and a small business owner who can be your mentor. After all, starting a micro business is not just about making money, it is about learning something too! These people will help you spot the weaknesses in your plan—they will help you to be successful!

What if you do not know an accountant? Visit my website **MicroBusinessForTeens.com** and send me an email. I will evaluate your business plan for a reasonable fee (include it in your start up expenses as a tax deduction!)

What if you do not know a business owner to be a mentor? Visit the SCORE website **SCORE.org/young.html.** SCORE has retired executives who volunteer their time to help small business start-ups. They even have a special focus on what they call "young entrepreneurs."

Important Points

- A business plan can help you anticipate anything that might go wrong.

- A business plan for a micro business can be quite short and simple.

- A business plan has three sections

1. Business Concept
   Description of the product or service
   Description of the industry
   How to measure success

2. Marketing Plan
   Potential customers
   Describe the competition
   Market surveys
   Risks

3. Financial Plan
   Start up Expenses
   Cost of your product or service
   Price you will charge customers
   Break even analysis
   Projected Income Statement

Example Business Plan
for
Emily's Piano Teaching Business

Business Concept

Product or Service: *Giving piano lessons*

Describe your product or service: *I will teach beginning piano students in a half-hour weekly lesson from my home.*

What makes your product or service unique? *I really like kids, and they seem to like me. I will charge about half the price of adult piano teachers. I will teach only beginners.*

Describe the industry and explain the need for your product or service: *Most children take music lessons at some point in their life and most start with piano as their first instrument. The market is huge and parents are willing to spend money on piano lessons.*

What are new trends in your industry? *New methods, fun games on the computer*

Is there opportunity for you in your industry? *Yes!*

How will you measure success? Will it be a financial goal or based on sales or number of customers? *I would be successful if I had 5 students that liked me enough to continue after three months.*

Define with numbers ($, people or sales units) your goal: *I hope to earn a little spending money, maybe $100 a month.*

What do you hope to learn by starting this micro business? *I want to learn how to teach children. I want to see if I would like being a piano teacher professionally.*

What knowledge, experience and skills do you possess that will be helpful in your business? *I have been taking piano lessons for 10 years. I really like working with children.*

What knowledge do you lack? *Piano teaching methods, running a business, marketing, billing parents, and record keeping.*

List an accountant that can help you: *My mother is a CPA*
List a lawyer that can help you: *Not needed*
List an insurance agent that can help you: *Not needed*
List an experienced business owner that can help you: *My current piano teacher*

What licenses and permits are required to operate your business? *None, according to my CPA.*
I will use my name, not a business name. I will use my personal checking account and will not apply for an EIN. Zoning laws permit me to have one client at a time.

Emily's Piano Teaching Business

Marketing Plan

Customers

Who are your potential customers? *Beginning piano students between 5 and 10 years old*

How will you reach potential customers? Where will you find them? *I will start with my homeschool co-op parents and kids in my neighborhood. I will ask my mom to tell her friends. I could put out an electronic ad on our homeschool forum or e-mail my parents' friends.*

How much will you spend (in time and money) doing advertising? Be as specific as possible and include website costs if you will create one. *No website needed. I may spend 2-3 hours sending e-mails looking for students at the start. I won't spend any extra money.*

Competition

Who is your competition? *Experienced piano teachers*

What are your competitors' strengths? What are your competitors' weaknesses? *Strengths: Experience. Sometimes a music degree. They are adults. Weaknesses: They will charge more. Some of them don't take beginners.*

How will you stand out? Why will people buy from you and not your competition? *I will charge half the going rate. I am personable and really like kids. Kids are less intimidated by me than by an adult teacher.*

Surveys

Tell at least five people about your product or service. Ask them: Would you buy from me? How much would you pay?

Record what they said:

Name	Would you buy from me?	What price?
1. *Mom*	*Yes*	*$10/lesson*
2. *Mrs. Lucas*	*Yes*	*$5/lesson*
3. *Mrs. Lamb*	*Yes*	*$7/lesson*
4. *Mrs. Tann*	*Yes*	*$6/lesson*

Risks

What are your major areas of risk? What can go wrong? *I won't be a good teacher. My inexperience will show. The kids won't like me. Students could cancel and not pay me.*

I could get sick and have to cancel a lesson. Parents might not like my methods. Students won't practice. Students might disobey me.

I might get too busy and have to quit teaching. My piano might break and I would have to quit teaching. I could break a finger and not be able to teach!

Emily's Piano Teaching Business

Financial Plan

Start Up Expenses

Equipment Needed	Parental Approval	Own or Need to Buy?	Cost to Buy
Piano	Yes	Own	$0.00

Space Needed	Parental Approval	Own or Need to Rent?	Cost to Rent Space
none			

What other startup expenses will you have? Get specific costs.

Item	Cost
Advertising	Free email
Professional advice	Free
Licenses and permits	None needed
Starting inventory	Music books for $20
Supplies	Reward stickers $5
Total Start Up Expenses	$25.00

Where will your initial funding come from? *My savings*

Item Cost

Fixed Costs	Amount each month (or year)
Piano tuning twice a year	*$180 a year*
Total Fixed Cost	*$180 per year*

Variable Costs	Amount per unit sold
none	

Profit
What profit do you hope to make on each item sold or customer serviced?
Almost 100% profit, since teaching piano has very few expenses.

Pricing:
What will you charge?
$7 for a 30-minute lesson

Is it reasonable?
Yes. I will still make $14/hour which is better than working in fast food or at the mall.

What do your competitors charge?
$15-$30 for a half-hour lesson

Sales

What are your estimated sales for the first three months, the next three months, and the first year? You can start with products sold or customers serviced, but then calculate the dollars of sales.

	Sales in units or customers	Sales in dollars
First 3 months sales	3 students	$21/week or $84/month
3-6 months sales	5 students	$35/week or $140/month
Sales for first year	At most 7 students	$200/month or $2,400/year

Break-Even Analysis

Break-even analysis is not applicable to services like piano lessons, but as an example, Emily wants to sell Beethoven T-shirts to her students. She can buy them for $5.50 each.

Add all the Fixed Costs (from above)
    Start Up Expenses:
    Equipment $0
    Space $0
    Other Fixed Costs: *$50 to the printer for the set up*

Total Fixed Costs for first year: *$50*
Total Variable Costs (from above): $*5.50*
Margin per unit = Selling Price per Unit – Variable Cost per Unit

$$= \$8.00 - \$5.50$$
$$= \$2.50 \ per \ unit$$

Break even point = Total Fixed Costs / Margin per Unit
                = *$50 / $2.50* per unit
                = *20* units
This is how many units you must sell in the first year to break even.

Is it reasonable?
No way! Twenty shirts when Emily has only five students! Forget the shirt idea!

Projected Income Statement for First Year

Emily expects seven students a week for about 40 weeks a year, allowing breaks for vacation and holidays.

Income
        Sales   *$2,000*

Cost of Goods Sold   *none for a service business*

Gross Profit   *$2,000*

Expenses (list separately)
        Start Up Costs $25
        Advertising
        Professional advice
        Supplies
        Piano Tuning   *$180*
Total Expenses $ 205

Net Income $ 1,795

Product Businesses Example

Emily had a service business, which can be very simple to manage financially. On the other hand, if you have some products to sell, the finances get more complicated. Here is a portion of the financial section of the business plan for a micro business that sells products.

Ted cares for dogs and cats when the owners are away. He also wants to expand his business and sell a few products.

> Doggie biscuits. Ted thinks he can sell 100 bags this year at $10 each. He has done some research and calculates that it will cost him $4.75 to make and package a box of doggie biscuits.

> Cat Chow. Ted thinks he can sell 200 bags of Cat Chow this year at $7 each. He has done some research and calculates that it will cost him $3.25 to make and package a bag of Cat Chow.

> Electronic book titled *How to Pet Sit for Fun and Money*. Ted knows from a website that it will cost him $400 to get his eBook published, and he thinks he can sell 50 copies this year at $12 each.

Financial Plan
For
Ted's Pet Care Business

Ted filled in the gray area from his business plan after doing a lot of research. Then, he calculated his margin for each product and feels pretty happy with the profit he can make on each item ($5.75 for the biscuits; $3.25 for the chow and $12 for each eBook).

Ted also calculated his break even point and was thrilled that he can cover his fixed expenses with only a few sales of the Doggie Biscuits and the Cat Chow. The eBook will take 34 sales to break even, but that is okay with Ted; he thinks that he will sell 50 books.

Then, Ted totals his Sales, COGS, and Gross Profit. He is pretty happy with the figures. It looks impressive to see a Gross Profit from his products of $1,825!

		Doggie Biscuits	Cat Chow	EBook	Total
1	Sales in 1 year	100	200	50	
2	Selling Price per unit	$10.00	$7.00	$12.00	
3	Variable Cost per unit	$4.25	$3.75	$0.00	
4	Fixed Costs	$50.00	$50.00	$400.00	$500.00
5	Margin per unit	$5.75	$3.25	$12.00	
6	Break Even units	8.7	15.38	33.33	
7	Total Sales	$1,000.00	$1,400.00	$600.00	$3,000.00
8	Total COGS	$425.00	$750.00	$0.00	$1,175.00
9	Gross Profit	$575.00	$650.00	$600.00	$1,825.00

Next, Ted completes his Projected Income Statement for his first year.

Income		
Sales of Products	$3,000.00 *Line 7 from the chart*	
Sales of Services (Pet Sitting)	$800.00	
Total Income	$3,800.00	
Cost of Goods Sold	-$1,175.00 *Line 8 from the chart*	
Gross Profit	$2,625.00	
Expenses		
Start Up Costs	$500.00 *Line 4 from the chart*	
Advertising	$45.00	
Professional advice	$50.00	
Other	$100.00	
Total Expenses	$695.00	
Net Income	$1,930.00	

As you can see, his income statement includes income from the product sales and his regular pet-sitting service. There are some additional expenses, like advertising and professional advice that Ted plans to pay in his first year (very smart of Ted to get some professional advice in the beginning!). All in all, Ted looks like he has a great plan and will have $1,930 of profit at the end of the year.

Chapter Five
Financing Your Business
Without Breaking the Bank

Start Your Micro Business Without Debt

Most of the books written for small business start ups include a chapter on financing. They include advice on how to get a loan, where to find angel investors or venture capital. These books also gear most of the business plan to pleasing a loan officer at a bank. None of this is necessary for a micro business owner, because a micro business can be started without any debt.

I encourage you to carefully consider what it will take financially to start your micro business. You may find that you are not ready to launch a particular idea yet because you lack the money. In that case, I recommend that you start a smaller micro business and save up the profits to use when you launch your more expensive business.

What Do You Need to Start?

Did you make out a business plan in Chapter Four? If you did, turn to the Financial Plan section of your business plan and record the information on start-up expenses below. If you did not create a business plan, you are getting ahead of yourself. Go prepare that plan! At the very least, fill in the data on start-up expenses.

> Lucas wanted to start a micro business mowing lawns. He wanted a riding lawnmower for the business, but didn't have enough money. So instead Lucas worked delivering papers and eventually bought a riding lawnmower at a garage sale. His lawn mowing business is now quite successful and was started debt free!

Start –up Expenses

What start-up equipment is needed? Will you need a computer, a desk, or an oven? Where will it come from? Does your family already own the equipment? Ask your parents' permission to use it! Will you need to buy some equipment? What will it cost to purchase?

Equipment Needed	Parental Approval	Own or Buy?	Cost to purchase

Calculating your start-up expenses may not be easy for you. Do a search on the internet or your local stores to gather prices. Do not guess; rather get accurate information. Show your list to your parents, a mentor or your accountant for their opinions. They can be your reality check.

No Money Down

Some micro businesses can be launched without any start-up expenses at all. You can often use the equipment and tools you (or your family) already own. Things like:

- a piano or guitar to teach lessons
- a stove and oven to cook food
- a vacuum cleaner and mop to clean houses
- your two feet to walk dogs
- your babysitting training to do childcare
- your computer to do web design

The Problems With Debt

Most micro businesses do not require a lot of start up funds, making them an attractive way to launch a business. Some teenagers even start micro businesses as a means to fund another, larger business. Try to start your micro business without any debt. Then, all your profits can go back into the business or, better yet, your pocket!

There are several reasons why I discourage starting a micro business with debt and I have collected some great quotes to back me up, most from the Bible, but plenty of others have advice to give about avoiding debt.

- Debt presumes upon the future. You are taking a risk, or making a bet, that you will have money in the future that you do not have today and that presumption is dangerous. None of us knows what lies ahead, and it is risky to assume that we can predict the future.

Why, you do not even know what will happen tomorrow. What is your life? You are a mist that appears for a little while and then vanishes.

The Bible, James 4:14

- The use of debt or borrowing encourages quick or rash decisions. If you quickly get a loan, you will not take the necessary time to consider other funding methods or be creative in finding needed money or equipment. Careful planning and making decisions after a lot of careful thought can pay off financially. Taking your time can also help you avoid many mistakes.

Careful planning puts you ahead in the long run; hurry and scurry puts you further behind.

The Bible, Book of Proverbs 21:5

He that goes a borrowing goes a sorrowing.
Benjamin Franklin

- Being in debt makes you a slave to the lender. When you owe a debt, you are not free; you are under obligation to another person for the loan. Debt creates a burden that will drag you and your business down.

> *The rich rule over the poor, and the borrower*
> *is slave of the lender*
> The Bible, Book of Proverbs 22:7

- Taking on debt increases your risk of failure. Your first profits must go toward paying off the loan instead of back into your business to help it grow. You may be able to pay back the debt, only to find your business is dead.

> *When a man is in love or in debt, someone else*
> *has the advantage.*
> Bill Balance, radio talk show host

- Debt can stop blessings. Turning to a loan can deny God the ability to bless you or to bring other people in to help you. There are people willing to help with free items, advice or even money, if you will only ask.

> *Neither a borrower nor a lender be;*
> William Shakespeare, *Hamlet* Act 1, scene 3

Our refrigerator died four days before the new one was to be delivered. I could have spent $100 to purchase a mini fridge to get us by for a few days, but I didn't want another appliance. Instead of rushing out to the store and using my credit card, I called a few neighbors and friends. In only a few hours, I had borrowed two mini refrigerators that met my needs without using any cash. Neighbors and friends were more than willing to help.

Where Will the Money Come From?

If you do need some cash to start, here are some tried and true methods.

- Save the money first. Many small business owners think they need a loan to start a business, but that is not necessarily true for micros. A loan only drains your profit instead of helping to save toward your goal. Rather than getting a loan, save up some money first. Consider it paying yourself first. If you could pay back a loan, you should be able to save up some money beforehand. Some business owners believe that the business will pay for itself, but since most businesses fail, that belief can lead to financial ruin. Saving up the cash first is better than going into debt.

- Start as a hobby. You can run your micro as a hobby without the goal to earn a profit, but to break even by just covering your expenses at first. You will learn a lot about marketing, pricing your product or service and expenses. You will not have the burden of trying to make a profit because your goal is to learn a lot. Later, you can take what you have learned to launch another, larger business that will generate a profit.

- Find an investor, but not a partner. Investors are willing make a loan to a new business and may not expect to be repaid for a long period, if ever. Investors could be your parents, grandparents, or a business mentor.

> Matthew Rushton borrowed $100 from his parents to start his knife selling business at the age of twelve. He paid back his parents with his first profits.

In general, I discourage partnerships because they are like being married without being in love. In a partnership, you are legally responsible for any debt or obligation to which your partner agrees. A teenage micro business owner should not put him or herself into a situation where they could be responsible for another person's actions. A partnership should be a written agreement reviewed by an attorney.

At the same time, partnerships can be formed by a *verbal* agreement, so be very careful about what you say or promise to another person.

Most legal agreements entered into by teenagers are full of risk because common law has long held that minors lack the maturity of mind or judgment to enter into a contract. I am sorry about that negative view of teenagers as being immature. (I know there are exceptions). However, but stay away from partnerships until you are over 18 years old and have a good attorney.

Phil and his best friend, Brian, verbally agreed to start a partnership and split everything 50/50. The business really took off and was generating over $1,000 a month in income.

Brian's father saw how successful the business had become and claimed the business was solely Brian's business and not a partnership. Phil ended up discussing the matter with an attorney and eventually lost money on the situation, but he gained a lot of wisdom and caution. He and Brian are no longer best friends, as you can imagine.

Later, Phil started his own micro business as a wiser sole proprietorship and was phenomenally successful.

- Sell something to raise cash. If you have a valuable possession such as a musical instrument, electronics or a collectible, raise cash by selling it. Have a garage sale, post it to Craig's List or eBay and advertise it as a fund raiser to launch a new business. You will be advertising your business and raising money at the same time.

- Work a temporary job. Work retail over Christmas or deliver pizzas for a few months to earn some cash. You can practice the time management skills that you will need when you start your micro business.

> Lauren is a full time college student trying to launch a web-based retail store. She needs about $800 to start her business and buy inventory. Lauren plans to work during her breaks from college to earn the $800 in start up funds.

Any or all of these ideas to generate your start up cash might work for you. Just remember to keep your micro business manageable and as debt free as possible. Your goal is to learn a lot, not to go into debt.

Start Without Risk

Most small business books describe small business owners as entrepreneurs. However, entrepreneurs are described as risk-takers, driven, focused, daring, and so on. It is not necessary to be a risk-taker to be a micro business owner. Micro owners are in business to make money and learn something, but without losing their life or their money!

You can be a successful micro owner with minimal risk.

- Have a plan. In an earlier chapter I encouraged you to write up a business plan and have at least three people review it. I hope you did that and learned how to lessen the risk of failure by following the advice of your mentors. They do not mean to criticize you, but rather wish to see you succeed. A business plan will help you see where problems can arise and deal with them beforehand.

- Keep your expenses low. Run your business with as few expenses as possible as you begin. Try not to accumulate start-up expenses, but rather expand your business as profits come in. A smart micro owner will add more products to his or her product line as customers request them, but not before. Start small and manageable and expand when you can afford it.

- Avoid debt. I offered several suggestions to save up or work to earn start up funds. If you can avoid debt to start your micro business, a huge risk is lessened and you will be on your way to profitability very soon.

> Working at home means you can work at just about any hour of the day or night.
>
> E-mails from one of my teenage micro business clients were usually time stamped at midnight, 1:00 a.m., or later because that's when he worked on his web design business.

- Stay at home. Keep your business home-based as long as possible, maybe forever. There are so many advantages to running a business from your home such as free rent, no commute, no extra security or insurance problems, and you can be working at your business any time of day or night.

- Aim to learn a lot. One of your primary goals in starting a micro business should be to learn a lot. You may not even expect to make a profit, but desire to break even. List the things you hope to learn, such as marketing, pricing, customer service or controlling expenses. Aiming to learn a lot and not being focused on making a profit will lessen your risk.

Important Points

- Calculate your start-up expenses
- Use what you already own
- Save up the start up cash first
- Aim to break even
- Find an investor, but not a partner
- Sell something to raise cash
- Work a temporary job to earn start-up funds
- Avoid risk by:
    having a plan
    keep expenses low
    avoid debt
    stay home-based
    aim to learn a lot

Chapter Six
Taking Care of Business
Extra Information to Get You Started

In Chapter Two, Getting an Idea, I shared a lot of ideas for a micro business. There was not room in that chapter to share with you all the extra information you may need to get started in a particular business. This chapter will fill in that gap.

Depending on your business, you should start by reading about your particular industry, service, or product. For example, if you are planning to do some babysitting, you should read about baby care and child development. Try and do your research and reading for as little money as possible. Your local library is a good place to start and naturally a Google search will uncover a lot of information.

Another good place to start is my website, **MicroBusinesforTeens.com**. I post information there on specific micro businesses, so you can learn tips and the traps of popular business ideas.

Home-based Business Series

I was so happy to find this *Home-based Business* series from Globe Pequot. They have dozens of titles and most of them work perfectly for teenage micro business owners. The books are written by people who have actually run these business, so you get real life, practical advice. Many update their versions every couple of years, so be sure you have the latest and greatest version.

> *How to Start a Home-Based Writing Business* by Lucy V. Parker
> *How to Start a Home-Based Online Retail Business* by Jeremy Shepherd
> *How to Start a Home-Based Photography Business* by Kenn Oberrecht
> *How to Start a Home-Based Handyman Business* by Terry Meany
> *How to Start a Home-Based Catering Business* by Denise Vivaldo
> *How to Start a Home-Based Professional Organizing Business* by Dawn Noble
> *How to Start a Home-Based Jewelry Making Business* by Maire Loughran
> *How to Start a Home-Based Web Design Business* by Jim Smith
> *How to Start a Home-Based Gift Basket Business* by Shirley George Frazier
> *How to Start a Home-Based Craft Business* by Kenn Oberrecht
> *How to Start a Home-Based Landscaping Business* by Owen Dell

How to Start a Home-Based Event Planning Business by Jill Moran, CSEP
How to Start a Home-Based Housecleaning Business by Laura Jorstad and Melinda Morse

Babysitting

Some of the best training to be a babysitter is to take a Safe Sitter class (find a local class at **http://www.safesitter.org**) or a Red Cross Babysitter Training course. The Red Cross website has helpful forms to use on a babysitting job. Google "Red Cross babysitting" for the correct website.

"Your Teenager's Babysitting Business" by Terrie Lynn Bittner offers great tips for a teenager starting a babysitting business such as having a surprise bag of toys, how to impress parents, and what to do in an emergency.
Read the article at
http://www.suite101.com/article.cfm/parenting_teenagers/40963/1.

Babysitters have some tax advantages. If you go to someone's house to babysit, you are considered a household employee. Household employees under age 18 do not have to pay Social Security or Medicare taxes. See my book *Teens and Taxes: A Guide for Parents and Teenagers* at **http://TeensAndTaxes.com** for details.

Cleaning and De-Cluttering

No one really likes cleaning, so try and get it done as fast as you can, collect your pay, and get on with your life! *Speed Cleaning* by Jeff Campbell from **TheCleanTeam.com** will help you cut your cleaning time in half. Really! I bought his book and video and cleaning takes a lot less time than it used to.

TheCleanTeam.com has a great system to control clutter too. *Clutter Control* by Jeff Campbell can help you learn the tricks to launch a de-cluttering business.

Realize that some people who hoard stuff have an emotional problem that is beyond your ability to fix. Read up about hoarders so you can tell the difference between a person in need of professional help and just a person who want to de-clutter. *Digging Out: Helping Your Loved One Manage Clutter, Hoarding, and Compulsive Acquiring* by Michael Tompkins is a good place to start.

Food Preparation

Food preparation can be a great micro business for a teenager who loves to bake, grill, or cook. However, be very careful about food preparation. It is very easy for something to go wrong and have food spoil. You do not want to be responsible for sickness or food poisoning. Because of the safety issues around food, most state and local governments have a lot of regulations and rules.

Do a lot of reading before you start preparing food for

sale.

Extension Offices Have Information

There are several zoning and health regulations when preparing food for resale, so check with your local cooperative extension office to learn your local area regulations. A cooperative extension office is an organization that is an extension of a state department of agriculture and a state university. Cooperative extension offices also have oversight of 4-H programs. Their offices have experts who share useful, practical information to small business owners, youth, and consumers. Visit this website to find a Cooperative Extension office near you: **http://NIFA.usda.gov/Extension**.

Find the contact person in your county. Call this person and say,

> *"I'm a teenager wanting to start a business selling* _____ *(cookies or whatever food your want to sell) that I bake in my home. Can you help me understand what the required licenses and permits would be?"*

Ask for information to be mailed to you or ask for an Internet link. Get information in writing so you can refer to it later. Extension employees, usually ladies as sweet as your grandmother, are extremely helpful. If you are too shy to call, then e-mail your question.

Examples of Food Safety Laws

Here's an example of food preparation regulations from Michigan.:

Food Regulations for Small Home Business [1] by Mary D. Zehner, Extension Specialist in Agricultural Economics

Many people make plans to open a food related small home business but are quite surprised by the number of laws and regulations that apply to their situation. Before you go too far into planning a food related small home business there are certain things you need to know.
A license from the Michigan Department of Agriculture (MDA) is needed for each location for the processing, storage and/or selling of packaged or unpackaged food, food ingredients and/or drinks for human consumption. Any exceptions to the licensing regulation are noted.
    Baked goods
    Bottled water
    Cake decorating
(*Several more are listed. Visit the website if you live in Michigan for details.*)
[1] http://web1.msue.msu.edu/imp/modi2/09159436.html

Michigan lets you make baked goods without a license, so that's good news for teenage micro business owners.

Iowa allows baked goods to be made at home and sold to the public, but you need a home food establishment license. Your business is exempt from the license if you produce non-potentially hazardous food such as baked goods that do not need refrigeration after preparation. Visit **http://www.extension.iastate.edu/Publications/PM1294. pdf** for details.

Colorado has a very helpful website with common questions and answers at
http://www.jeffco.us/health/health_T111_R45.htm

I want to make food in my home and sell it. How do I get a food service license? A licensed kitchen is required; this must be separate from your household kitchen. A restaurant kitchen may be rented during off-hours, or some church kitchens are properly equipped and can be used. This department must approve your planned location and then provide an application for a food service license. A plan review packet may be obtained through this office. A Colorado sales tax license must be obtained prior to this department issuing a food service license. You should also check with your local zoning department about the legality of home businesses in your area.

I want to do catering from my home, can I do that? No food preparation for a catered event can occur in your household kitchen. If you are purchasing the food items and taking them to the location of the catered event for preparation, then no food service license is required.

As you can see, Colorado wants you to have a sales tax license and a food service license before you start selling your food items. If you live in Colorado, you should contact the local cooperative extension office to see if there are exceptions to these regulations.

These examples are to give you an idea of some common food preparation regulations. You need to call your local cooperative extension office (website given above) to get information on your local regulations.

House Sitter

If you are a dependable, trustworthy person, you may be hired to "house sit" or care for a house while the owner is away.

HouseCarers.com **http://www.housecarers.com** has a book, "Guide to House Sitting", articles, and a blog.

Lawn Care

Mowing grass and shoveling snow are really great businesses for teenagers. They are easy to start, use tools like a mower and shovel that you may already own and a teenager can make money right in his neighborhood. A lawn care business comes with some tax benefits too. See my website, **TeensandTaxes.com,** to learn about the tax benefits of being what the IRS calls a "household employee."

Here are a few websites and books written by other lawn care business owners that pass along what they know. There can be a lot more to lawn care than just mowing grass!

> *TeenLawnCare.com.* Ben tells of his experience in lawn care on this blog. Helpful articles include "Weed Eater Safety," "Dealing with Dog's You-know-what," "Raking Leaves," and "Snow Shoveling." He also lists other lawn care sites and forums.
>
> *Official Junior Biz Lawn Mowing Guide* by Nick Tart

and   Emil   Motycha.   Available   at **http://www.JuniorBiz.com** (paperback or eBook). This is a short book, but packed with very helpful information from teenagers who know the business.

How to Start Your Own Lawn Care Business. Daniel Pepper sells an eBooks for $47. At his blog he offers   tips   and   inspiration: **http://www.howtostartyourlawncarebusiness.c om/articles/**.

Pet Sitting

Pet sitting is a great micro business for animal lovers. Here are some websites to get you started.

Pet Sitters.biz at **http://www.pet-sitters.biz** has a long list of articles and a helpful blog with answers to common questions such as handling aggressive dogs and how to tell if a pet is sick.

Pet Sitters International at **http://www.petsit.com/** sells a start up kit ($125 for a book, DVD, and marketing materials) and even T-shirts to promote your business.

Self Publishing

You know something about some *thing* don't you? Well then, write it down and tell the world. Write and self-publish your own eBook. In this day of self-publishing and electronic books, it is so fast and easy to share your knowledge and get paid for it.

Here are some websites to get you started in the world of self-publishing:

Nick Tart started mowing grass when he was 12 years old. Now he has written an eBooks about it called *The Official Junior-Biz Lawn Mowing Guide.*

Christopher Paolini was 15 when he self published *Eragon* before it was picked by Knopf, a large publishing house. It is now a best selling novel and movie.

CreateSpace.com is a simple way to get a book published. You can also create and sell videos, DVDs, CDs and audio downloads.

Lulu.com revolutionized the world of publishing by helping the little guy get a book published. I use them myself for short print runs of my eBooks. They are great, easy to use, and fun!

Cindy Rushton is a self-publishing expert with over 100 titles and is my personal mentor when it comes to self-publishing. Check out her website, **CindyRushton.com,** for information on her online classes and podcasts (some with me as a guest!). Cindy is very inspirational and will motivate you to get that book out. She'd be thrilled to work with an aspiring teenage author who has something to say!

Information in a Nutshell: Writing and Publishing by Felice Gerwitz is a compact book (only 127 pages), that is packed with information on getting started as an author and self-publishing your book. Available at **http://www.mediaangels.com/**.

Sewing

www.BunkhouseSewing.com has patterns and *lots* of ideas for a sewing business such as Halloween costumes, church banners, doll clothes, holiday placemats, baby slings, etc. You could also consider teaching younger people (usually girls) how to sew. The website owner, JoAnn Gagnon, has a very inexpensive eBook on teaching sewing as a business, *Teaching Sewing FAQs Answered* for $3.95. You can also visit Joan's blog or sign up for her newsletter of sewing tips.

Web Design

Web design is a popular idea for micro businesses. You may have to do some studying to learn about html and CSS code, search engine optimization or how to set up a blog, but it is a fun and creative business to run.

Wordpress.org is a blog platform that many websites use to build a website. All of my websites are built on the Wordpress platform. It is easy to learn and to use. You can learn about Wordpress from tutorial videos on their website or at **YouTube.com**.

WebsiteTips.com is an educational resource especially for Web designers, teachers and educators, and students. There are tutorials, recommended books, and tons of links to the best resources for starting a web design business.

There is no shortage of websites and eBooks on web design. Start with free resources such as your library and free tutorials on the web. After you have a basic understanding of web design, you could invest in some paid classes or books.

Important Points

- Read a lot to learn from others who have started a business.

- Your local library is a great place to start.

- An internet search will offer a lot of information on your specific area of business.

- The websites mentioned in this chapter are only a beginning. Never stop learning!

Chapter Seven
Encouragement
Final Words to Motivate You

This short book on starting a micro business is enough to get you started with an idea and a plan for it to be successful. You have what you need to get started, but you don't know everything you need to know just yet. Fortunately, with a micro business, you can learn as you go. My website, **MicroBusinessForTeens.com**, will answer your questions, offer stories and give advice.

There are also more books to follow this one. *Running a Micro Business* covers sales, marketing, customer service, record keeping, and time management. *Money and Taxes in a Micro Business* covers income taxes, tax deductions, sales tax, employees and working with an accountant. Both books are available at **MicroBusinessFor-Teens.com**.

I don't think much of a man who is not wiser today than he was yesterday.
Abraham Lincoln

Keep It Manageable

Do not be overwhelmed by the thought of starting a business. If you don't like it, you can shut it down. If you get busy with school or sports, you can stop taking customers. You can control how much or how little you put into your business.

Obviously, the more you put into your business with your time and effort, the more you will gain in return. You will earn more money, but you will also learn a lot about running a business and about yourself as well.

Learning Has Benefits

You go into business to make money, but wouldn't it be great if your business also had other benefits? What if you learned so much, you decided to launch another, larger business? What if you found your future career by running a micro business?

Meghan taught violin lessons to children when she was a teenager. She loved playing violin and enjoyed teaching so much that she decided to study violin in college. Running her micro business helped her find her future career.

Hold on to instruction, do not let it go; guard it well, for it is your life.
The Bible, Book of Proverbs 4:13

Or what if you learned what you definitely do *not* want to do for a career? What would that be worth to you? Starting a micro business can be a huge learning experience, without paying tuition.

You Can Do This

This book is full of stories from real-life teenagers who started micro businesses. You may never read about them on a blog or news story. They are just normal kids, trying to make a little money, learn about a business and themselves, and keep up with their homework. These micro business owners may never be famous or super rich, but they are helping people, earning money, and discovering what they want to do in life. They may not even consider themselves entrepreneurs; they are just teenagers with an idea of how to make some money.

If they can do it, so can you!

Find an Encourager

Be sure to find someone who can encourage you to get started and stick with your micro business for a while. That person might be your parents, an adult business owner, or another teenager that runs a micro business.

Some people find great encouragement from successful business owners. You might want to read biographies of famous business owners such as:

My daughter Emily inspired another girl, Julieann, to start offering piano lessons. She followed Emily's example and taught only a few beginner piano students. The students loved her and so did the parents because Julianne did not charge as much as the adult piano teachers.

Mary Kay Ash, founder of Mary Kay cosmetics
Donald Trump, real estate millionaire
Dan Cathy, the owner of Chick-Fil-A
Dave Thomas, founder of Wendy's.

You might also want to read *Conversations with Teen Entrepreneurs* by Ben Cathers and *50 Interviews: Young Entrepreneurs. What It Takes to Make More Money Than Your Parents* by Nick Scheides and Nick Tart.

I also share profiles on teenage micro business owners at **MicroBusinessForTeens.com**

Persevere and Press On

Don't give up too easily. You will probably find some part of running a micro business difficult or unpleasant. That is not a reason to quit, but instead a reason to press on. Eventually, you may find a way to get past the difficulty and you will feel a surge of confidence and success.

One of my favorite sayings about perseverance is from the Bible and it says:

> *We also rejoice in our sufferings, because we know that suffering produces perseverance; perseverance, character; and character, hope.*
> The Bible, Book of Romans 5:3,4

You, like me, may not like the idea of "rejoicing in our sufferings," but I like the ending where eventually we get hope. Sometimes it is only through trials and difficulties that we learn something new and have a door opened up to us for new things.

> I didn't know how to create a website and it was a road block to success in a new business project. So I signed up for an on-line class and learned how to create a website using a Word-press blog as the platform. It turned out to be fun and pretty easy. I was so thrilled when someone complimented my site (**TeensAndTaxes.com**) and asked who my web designer was! Instead of feeling like a quit-ter when I ran into a difficulty, I felt confident and proud of my efforts.

Share Your Story

If you start a micro business, don't keep it to yourself. Tell someone! Tell me (email me at my website, **MicroBusi-nessForTeens.com**), tell your friends, tell your grand-mother and tell the world on Facebook or on your blog. It is not bragging to say, "I am starting a new business." It is an inspiration to other people that they, too, can start a micro business.

When you share your story, it encourages you to try a bit harder. When people go on a diet to lose weight they are encouraged to tell everyone they know. Why? It helps to keep them accountable on their diet. The same idea can work for you. Tell people you are trying to launch a busi-ness and it can be a motivation for you to work hard.

Do not be afraid of failure. You cannot fail with a micro business; you just learn something that didn't work. You will know to try something different next time.

> *I have not failed, not once. I've discovered ten thousand ways that don't work.*
> Thomas Edison, who tried thousands of experiments to invent the light bulb.

So go ahead and get started, even if you only have one customer. Then tell me your story. What did you try and what did you learn? I look forward to hearing from you!

About the Author

Carol Topp, CPA, owner of **CarolToppCPA.com** and **MicroBusinessForTeens.com,** helps people, especially teenagers, start their own small businesses.

Carol was born and raised in Racine, Wisconsin and graduated from Purdue University with a degree in engineering. She worked ten years for the US Navy as a cost analyst before staying home with her two daughters. While being a stay-at-home mom, Carol took accounting classes via distance learning. In 2000, Carol received her CPA license and opened her own practice.

She is a member of the Ohio Society of CPAs, the National Association of Tax Professionals, and the Society of Nonprofit Organizations. Carol has presented numerous workshops on money management, business start-up, taxes, and budgeting to various community, church, and homeschool groups.

She has authored several books including:
- *Homeschool Co-ops: How to Start Them, Run Them and Not Burn Out*
- *The IRS and Your Homeschool Organization*
- *Information in a Nutshell: Business Tips and Taxes for Writers*
- *Teens and Taxes: A Guide for Parents and Teenagers*

And several magazine articles in
- *The Old Schoolhouse*
- *Home Education*
- *Homeschool Enrichment*
- National Association of Tax Professionals *TaxPro*
- *Nonprofit World*

Carol lives in Cincinnati, Ohio with her husband and two daughters where she runs her micro business from her home.

If you enjoyed *Starting a Micro Business,* look for other books in the Micro Business for Teens series.

Running a Micro Business covers record keeping, inventory, selling products, time management, marketing and customer service.

Money and Taxes in a Micro Business covers financial statements, income taxes, tax deductions, sales tax, employees and working with an accountant.

Micro Business for Teens Workbook is designed for individual or group study. Put into practice what you read in *Starting a Micro Business* and *Running a Micro Business*.

Also available are audios, virtual classes, webinars, and video instruction on starting and running a micro business.

Available at **MicroBusinessForTeens.com**